LIGHTNING
BOLT
BOOKS™

T0015917

Haunted Places

Susan B. Katz

Lerner Publications ◆ Minneapolis

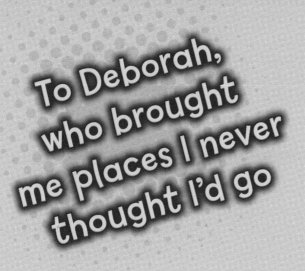

To Deborah, who brought me places I never thought I'd go

Lerner Publications Company
An imprint of Lerner Publishing Group, Inc.
241 First Avenue North
Minneapolis, MN 55401 USA

For reading levels and more information, look up this title at www.lernerbooks.com.

Main body text set in Billy Infant Regular. Typeface provided by SparkType.

Photo Editor: Annie Zheng
Lerner team: Sue Marquis

Library of Congress Cataloging-in-Publication Data

Names: Katz, Susan B., 1971- author.
Title: Haunted places / Susan B. Katz.
Description: Minneapolis, MN : Lerner Publications , [2024] | Series: Lightning bolt books ® - that's scary! | Includes bibliographical references and index. | Audience: Ages 6-9 | Audience: Grades 2-3 | Summary: "Readers are in for some delicious thrills when they read about locales where ghosts are said to dwell, from haunted houses and hotels to creepy castles and spooky landmarks"— Provided by publisher.
Identifiers: LCCN 2022039613 (print) | LCCN 2022039614 (ebook) | ISBN 9781728491189 (library binding) | ISBN 9798765603321 (paperback) | ISBN 9781728498706 (ebook)
Subjects: LCSH: Haunted places—Juvenile literature. | Ghosts—Juvenile literature.
Classification: LCC BF1461 .K39 2024 (print) | LCC BF1461 (ebook) | DDC 133.1—dc23/eng/20221017

LC record available at https://lccn.loc.gov/2022039613
LC ebook record available at https://lccn.loc.gov/2022039614

Manufactured in the United States of America
1-53049-51067-12/12/2022

Table of Contents

Spooky!

Have you ever been to a haunted house? Haunted houses are homes where ghosts are said to live.

Hotels, castles, and other places can be haunted too. In haunted places, things may move on their own. Doors could slam shut. Spooky figures might appear in mirrors.

Haunted Hotels

A room in California's Queen Anne Hotel is said to have a friendly ghost. Guests claim the ghost looks after them. She even tucks them in at night!

The Lizzie Borden House in Fall River, Massachusetts

Some say the Lizzie Borden House is a haunted inn. Borden was accused of killing her dad and stepmom. She was found not guilty. But legend says she haunts the inn.

The 1886 Crescent Hotel and Spa gives ghost tours.

The 1886 Crescent Hotel and Spa in Arkansas was once a hospital. Many very ill patients died there. People claim the ghosts of these patients haunt the hotel.

San Antonio, Texas, has a haunted hotel. Workers and guests at the Emily Morgan Hotel have reported doors closing by themselves. They hear spooky noises and see ghosts roaming around.

Would you visit the Emily Morgan Hotel?

Creepy Castles

Leap Castle in Ireland was home to the O'Carrolls, a powerful Irish family. Visitors report seeing spirits there, such as the dagger-holding Red Lady. There's also a room called the Bloody Chapel in this creepy castle.

Dragsholm Castle in Denmark has a ghost called the White Lady. Her skeleton was found in the building, dressed in white. She fell in love with a commoner, so her dad locked her in the castle. Now she's said to haunt it.

The White Lady is just one of Dragsholm Castle's ghosts.

People claim to hear eerie bagpipe music at Edinburgh Castle.

Edinburgh Castle in Scotland is home to many spirits. The music of a piper who disappeared long ago can be heard there. There are rumors of a headless drummer too!

Japan's Himeji Castle dates back to 1333. A story says an evil samurai there framed a servant named Okiku for losing an expensive plate. He killed her and threw her body down a well. Her ghost rises from the well counting plates!

There are many versions of Okiku's story, but all of them involve a well.

Ghostly Landmarks

Alcatraz was once a prison on a California island. The ghost of famous prisoner Al Capone is said to play the banjo in the shower there. People hear clanging and shouting in the former prison too.

The Lincoln Park Zoo in Chicago, Illinois, used to be a cemetery. Now dead people are believed to walk around the zoo as ghosts!

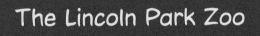
The Lincoln Park Zoo

The *Queen Mary*

The *Queen Mary* is docked in California. The ship originally came from England to the United States. About fifty people died on the ship. The spirits of those who've passed are thought to haunt it.

The Tower of London in England is believed to be haunted. One ghost there is Anne Boleyn. She was beheaded on the Tower grounds. Her ghost carries its head around!

Anne Boleyn was the Queen of England in the 1530s.

The lighthouse in St. Augustine, Florida, is a popular stop for ghost hunters. Two young, playful ghosts and one older, scary ghost are often seen there. People report hearing the playful ghosts giggling.

The scary lighthouse ghost wears blue and walks up and down the lighthouse stairs.

Share some fun and scary stories!

Do you believe in haunted places? Would you ever go to one? Real or not, the stories of these places are fun to read and share.

Fun Facts

- Stories say some ghosts move things around for fun. They might move books off a shelf or take food from the kitchen!

- Some fairs and theme parks have haunted houses. People visit them to get a fun scare.

- Some people say ghosts make lights flicker. Flickering lights are said to be a sign of a haunted building.

The Bissell Mansion

Captain Lewis Bissell built the Bissell Mansion in Missouri in about 1823. Now he's said to haunt the home. He and his wife Mary died there. There are reports of objects disappearing and a ghostly woman in white walking around. In 2022, the mansion went up for sale. Would you buy a haunted house?

Glossary

behead: to cut off someone's head

commoner: a common person, or someone who is not royalty

dagger: a sharp pointed knife

frame: falsely accuse

samurai: a member of the Japanese warrior class

spirit: a soul or a ghost

Learn More

Britannica Kids: Ghost
https://kids.britannica.com/kids/article/ghost/574605

Carlson-Berne, Emma. *Haunted History.* Minneapolis: Lerner Publications, 2024.

CBC Kids: 6 Spooky Things You Didn't Know about Ghosts
https://www.cbc.ca/kids/articles/monsters-101-all-about-ghosts

Kiddle: Ghost Facts for Kids
https://kids.kiddle.co/Ghost

Lassieur, Allison. *Scary Stuff.* Mankato, MN: Child's World, 2020.

Owings, Lisa. *Haunted Houses.* Minneapolis: Bellwether Media, 2019.

Index

Photo Acknowledgments

Image credits: Witthaya/iStock/Getty Images, p. 4; AlpamayoPhoto/E+/Getty Images, p. 5; fivepointsix/Shutterstock, p. 6; EQRoy/Shutterstock, p. 7; RaksyBH/Shutterstock, pp. 8, 9; Dirk Hudson/Shutterstock, p. 10; David Wall/Moment/Getty Images, p. 11; Away/Shutterstock, p. 12; Tsukioka Yoshitoshi/Wikimedia Commons PD, p. 13; Andrea Pistolesi/Stone/Getty Images, p. 14; Felix Mizioznikov/Shutterstock, p. 15; GagliardiPhotography/Shutterstock, p. 16; Photos.com/Getty Images, p. 17; Smithlandia Media/Moment Open/Getty Images, p. 18; Pixel-Shot/Shutterstock, p. 19.

Cover: Dirk Hudson/Shutterstock.